Home Business

By KC Tan

http://www.kctan.asia

CONTENTS

BONUS!

Before you continue, I would like to send you some free tools and resources to help you set up a profitable business from home.

Go to the following URL to get started!

http://homebusinesshelp.gr8.com/

NOTE FROM THE AUTHOR

First, I want to thank you for picking up this book and giving me this opportunity to share with you my experiences in starting a business from home. My guess is that you are considering to start your own business with as little investment as possible, if so, this is the right book for you.

I wrote this book for people who wanted to stop selling their time building businesses for others and instead, start building a meaningful and scalable business for themselves with minimum risk. One of the biggest advantages of working from home is that you can be assured that you do not need a lot of money to start. Unlike traditional businesses, where you need to invest capital in buying or renting a physical space, you can now better focus your money in the areas like marketing and customer services.

One of the strongest reasons that prevent people from starting their own business is that most people think that you need to have a lot of money to start a business. This is not true as I will share with you in this book, how you can sell first, then buy later. If you master this concept, you will never lose money in your business decisions in future.

I sincerely look forward to the day when you register and start a business from home. I believe this book will help you in many ways. If you are inspired to take actions after reading this book, I would be very happy because I have helped someone out there.

I also want to thank JJ&E for giving me their support all these years. I highly recommend that you check out http://www.jje.sg for all company registration and virtual office services.

I believe there are reasons why you are reading this book right now and I also believe that you deserve to live the entrepreneurial lifestyle you meant to be. No matter what immediate actions you take after reading my book, I wish you well and all the best!

Sincerely,

KC Tan

Home Business Coach

http://kctan.asia

INTRODUCTION

The main reason I write this book is to share my experiences and the things I have learned from the marketplace through the ups and downs of the economy in the past few years since I started my own business in 2008.

I realize many people around me have an idea that they wanted to start but don't really know how to get it started. I am always encouraging and supportive to my friends who wanted to start a business and break the 9 to 5 job cycle. But in most encounters, I do not have the luxury of time to share everything I know in a single session, so I thought of writing this book as a way to share my advice with more people who wants to start their businesses especially from the comfort of their homes.

Before reading this book, I sincerely hope that you will understand that in order for you to do the things that you haven't been doing, you need to adopt a new set of beliefs, mindset, and perspective. It is impossible for us to go from the employee to the self- employed lifestyle while still holding on to the old employee mindset.

A common employee mindset I want you to discard is "get paid by your time". Most employees get paid by working a certain amount of time in the organizations, and it is very common for you to continue thinking that the more you work, the more you will earn. This is simply wrong! Starting your own business requires you to have a totally new mindset where how much you earn will depend on how you maximize your resources and create leverage. I will share more about leverage in this book, for now, you just need to remind yourself every day that do not tag the money you earn to how much time you work! This new thinking will prepare you for business success!

After studying many successful business owners, I finally come to realization that in order to be successful in business, you need one of the two following traits:

Well Connected Or Creative

If you are already in the marketplace for years providing services or selling products, you will agree with me that some people are just well-connected and they are always 'lucky' to get closed door deals and opportunities. In order to be successful in business, one of the important traits is to have a well-connected network where you know some influential decision makers.

If you are not well-connected, you must be creative in order to be successful in business. When you are in the business, there will be ups and downs at different times of the market. When the market is down and it hurts your business, it will take creativity for you to break the down cycle of your business and make it profitable again. I remember back in 2009 where there were not many WordPress Instructors in Singapore, my WordPress classes are filling up quickly every month. After 2 to 3 years, as more and more people came out and teach WordPress, demand to my workshops decreases. That was the time I decided to teach WordPress for "free"! Yes, people actually come to my WordPress class for free, but on one condition, they need to host their websites on my server – where I will charge them a yearly hosting fee.

I was the first one in the market to do this, and every month, I have 20 to 30 people attending my free WordPress class and paying me for web hosting. From this example, you will notice that I switch my revenue model from training to web hosting but actually I still teach people how to use WordPress to create websites.

The good news is that if you are not well-connected or creative (yet) at the moment, these two traits can be cultivated and improved even before you start your business! This book will teach you how!

Of course, if you are well-connected and creative, you will definitely make tons of money and helping plentiful people in this marketplace!

But trust me; you do not need to have both traits! I have seen people who are well-connected but definitely not creative, and they have been making good money during the ups and downs of the market just because they know the influential people. If you need an example, just think of the construction field. A lot of construction companies they are not creative, and they keep doing the same thing for decades. The reason why they can still make money is because they have connections with the authority that issues the work orders.

Before we move on to the next chapter, ask yourself why do you need to start a home business now? Write down the top three reasons and always bear this in mind. I would like you to have a strong WHY before you proceed to read more in this book.

The last thing I want to help to shape your thinking is you don't really need to have a lot of money in order to start a home business! Whenever I have seminars and I ask the participants what are the main challenges for you to start a home business and the top reason people gave me is always not enough money!

With today's technologies, you wouldn't need a lot of money to gain visibility as compared to before where mass media is the only channel. Refer to the later chapter of the book where I teach you the concept of Sell First, Buy Later! There you will learn what a smarter way of making a business profitable is!

-

WHO'S KC?

Before we dive into the core sections of this book, allow me to introduce myself quickly so that you know more about me and perhaps can relate better to my sharing for the rest of this book.

My name is KC, and I started my business back in 2008. Back then, I was a Web Developer creating websites for small businesses. Actually, this is not what I wanted to do when I registered my business back then...

When I was holding a full-time job from 2006 to 2008, I was already helping some of my friends to create and optimize (through Search Engine Optimization) their websites online. While I was servicing my friends, I had an idea why not I start a tuition service where I will teach people Internet business rather than academic subjects like Mathematics and Science. I casually asked several of my friends about their thoughts on this idea and most of my friends said it is a brilliant idea!

But when I started my business offering this tutoring service, many people in the market do not know what I actually do. I spent the first three months looking for clients but ended up none. It was during these times where I changed my business model to Web Development because it is easier to understand for most people and I have no problems showing people my portfolio.

One of the defining moment for me and my business is when I met my business mentors in an Entrepreneurship course. One of my mentors his name is Ken Oon, and he introduces me to a business networking group called BNI (Business Network International). BNI has since changed my life because it has taught me how to grow my business and also gave me the referrals I needed to survive back then.

Another game-changer moment for me is when I met up with the boss of a secretariat company in Singapore. What they do is they help new companies register their businesses in Singapore, and they have a lot of walk-ins every day. So we form a collaboration, and they will refer all their customers to me to help them create their websites. This single one referral source contributes to more than 50% of my monthly sales!

As I create more and more websites for companies, I realize that it is even more important for the businesses to have the knowledge of maintaining their web marketing. Hence, I slowly changed my business model from creating websites for people, to teaching them how to create their websites.

It is not until 2014 where me and my wife decided to bring our training to online. Now, as I am writing this book, we are full-time working from home creating online courses. You can find all my courses listed on Udemy – https://udemy.com/u/kctan

Hopefully, after reading my story, you might realize that business ideas were not casted in stone. Along the way when you are in the marketplace finding and serving your clients, you will eventually change or improve your business model. This is very common. I urge you to remember that action is the key; it makes a lot of marketing plans irrelevant. The good thing is you can start by taking little actions before you even start your business. This book will teach you how.

I always believe that everyone of us has the Entrepreneurial blood and spirit inherited from our ancestors. It is just that through the formal education and upbringing environment that most of us lives in this era, it is not geared towards Entrepreneurial. But trust me, it is never too late to start. Colonel Harland Sanders founded KFC when he was 65. Charles Flint started IBM when he was 61. Joseph Campbell started Campbell Soup when he was 52. Every one of us has a chance, no matter how young or old we are!

I am proud to say that there has never been a better time in human history to work from home now especially with today's technology and most important, Internet.

-

THREE TYPES OF HOME BASED BUSINESSES YOU CAN START

There are generally three types of home based businesses that you can start. The first one is starting from scratch. This means you have an idea of selling a product or service and you go ahead to market them to your prospects.

If you start from scratch, you will have the most freedom because you are the one to decide everything from product development or service processes to marketing and supporting your customers. If you know clearly what you want to do, this mode of starting up is highly recommended!

The main advantage of starting from scratch is that you get to decide your own pricing and there is no other costs such as royalties to upkeep your business. The main disadvantage is that because of this freedom, you will have to setup your own process of selling, marketing, and customer support.

Now, do not be overwhelmed if you currently do not have experiences in sales, marketing and customer support. When I first started my business, I do not have this knowledge too. I pick up these skills along the way, and I believe you can do it too. It may seem like there are a lot of things to learn but put your focus on two things at the beginning; cashflow and great customer experience. Without cashflow, your business won't be able to survive long so you must quickly find an effective channel to get consistent sales for your business. And if you give great customer experiences every time, word of mouth will start to roll in after a few months. Hence remember, if you feel overwhelmed anytime, just shift the focus back to these two things – cashflow and great customer experiences.

The second way to start a home-based business is to buy a franchise. If you google for 'franchise direct', you will find the website (http://franchisedirect.com). You can search for a franchise that you can buy in your country and start running it as a business!

The advantage of buying a franchise is that you leverage the banding and the established process and system of the franchise. You do not need to think and create your own process of sales, marketing, and support. This will save you time from experimenting as well.

The disadvantage of buying a franchise is that you need to invest quite a bit of money before you start making money. And a lot of franchise requires you to pay annual royalties as well as a part of your revenue to upkeep your business.

I would only recommend franchise if you have a sum of money to invest and you truly love a particular business that currently has a franchise model.

The third way to start a business is via direct selling. Direct selling means that you sell a product or services to your friends or your friends' friends. However, you don't own the product or services, you are just a representative of a company. One example of such company is Amyway.

Many people called direct selling - multi-level marketing. I just want to clarify here that it is legal to run a multi-level marketing business especially if the company is registered with Direct Selling Association (http://dsa.org). However, it is illegal to run a pyramid scheme. Pyramid scheme means that there are no products or real services involved when customers make a purchase. You need to have a sharp eye to differentiate legitimate direct selling companies from the companies that have pyramid schemes. To be sure, you can check the direct selling association website to see if a company is listed as a member. If it is, then is a legitimate company that you can consider signing up as a Distributor.

The advantage of direct selling is that you can start this business with low cost. Most direct selling companies allow you to start a business with just a few hundred of dollars. They often provide training on how you can get sales as well.

The disadvantage of direct selling is that most people have negative experiences (especially in my country, Singapore) with multi-level marketing companies, so it is not easy to sell these products or services.

However, if you find that the product or service from the direct selling company is truly unique and add great value to people's lives, then I can recommend that you give it a try. I am sure you will learn a lot of valuable lessons in selling!

BUSINESS IDEAS YOU CAN START AT HOME!

In my experiences in the past few years, the following are the top most common businesses that start from home. If you do not have any idea of what businesses to start, perhaps you can find some inspiration below:

- Accountancy Services.

- Animator.

- Consultancy Services (IT, Management, Career, Education, Business, Marketing, etc.).

- Design / Advertising Services.

- Direct Sales (Direct Selling).

- eCommerce Online Stores.

- Event Planning.

- Game Development.

- Image Consultant.

- Infopreneur (this is what I do – creating information products).

- Jewelry Design.

- Knitting Products.

- Life Coach.

- Market Researcher.

- Personal Trainer.

- Photographer.

- Videographer.

- Retirement Planning.

- Self-Publishing.

- Translation Services.

- Travel Agent.

- Tutoring.

- Virtual Assistant Services.

- Web Development.

- Wedding Planning.

- Writer.

I hope that you can gain some inspiration or ideas from the above list of 26 professions.

These are all businesses that you can run from home. I have a friend, his name is Yong Sak, and he runs a photography business from home. He specializes in birthday parties' photography, and you can find his website at: http://yongsak.com.

I also have a few friends who provide accountancy services to businesses. Most of them are doing this part time as a business. If you are skilled in some ways, you can start by providing your services part-time and go full-time when volume picks up.

One of my friends, Mervyn Goh, he is a Web Designer specializes in creating websites for small businesses using WordPress which is an easy-to-use software that anyone can use. He started this business part-time and now doing full time. You can check out his website at: http://pegasusitsolution.com/

For me, I am an Infopreneur who creates informational products (eBooks, online courses, etc.) every month to help people start their online businesses. I have been doing this since 2008, and I am grateful that now I am running this business together with my lovely wife, Rachael.

Before I end this section, I want to encourage you to start something part-time before you go 100% full-time. The reason is because there are a lot of things to learn along the way and starting a business part-time will allow you to learn things with much lesser stress since your income does not depend on your new business alone.

Do not be too concerned that the first business you start may not be what you really want. Because the answer is, we will never know. It is very common for businesses to change their services scope along the way – this is how we learn. I have seen too many of my friends thinking about the "right" business for years and end up doing nothing for entire decade! Don't fall into the overthinking and overanalyzing trap. The most valuable lesson in life always comes from your realization when you start taking actions. Just to leave you with another part of my story.

When I was in university, I figured that I don't really want to work as an Electronic Engineer when I graduated, hence, I do something that interests in at that time – Game Development. I created an online game part-time during my final year in University. Later I got in the job where they look for IT Engineer, and I used my game development experiences to get myself landed in the job. It is from my game development experiences where I find that there is potential in online business and eventually leads me to today where I love to teach online. If you study this journey of mine, you will see that if I didn't create that online game, I would never figure out what I like to do today... Thus, I want to say that taking actions will eventually lead you to find out what you really meant to do in this lifetime.

THINGS YOU MUST KNOW BEFORE YOU START A HOME BASED BUSINESS!

This section covers some important things that I believe everyone should know before starting a business!

Give Your Business A Name!

First, you should give your business a professional name. The name that you came up with must be easy to remember, and if possible, people will know what you do just by seeing your company name.

However, you may not want to be very specific as well in case you need to change your scope of service in future. For example, if you provide name cards and other printing services and you name your company as "Alice Name Card Printing", people may not know that you provide other printing services. On top of this, if you decide to stop doing name cards printing in future, you will then need to change your company name. In this case, I would suggest that you just use "Alice Printing Services".

I also want to recommend you to write down a few possible names because you want to check if others have registered them before. If you are living in Singapore, you can check with ACRA online (google for BIZfile)for the existing names that are registered with the authorities.

Once you have checked that the name that you want to use is unique and no one has used before, the next step is to check if the domain name is available for you to register. A domain name is important for business because people will search online for your website to check out what services you have if they know about your company.

One good place to check if a domain name has been taken is namecheap.com. Take, for example, if you want to see if aliceprintingservices.com has been taken, you can just type in this domain name into the search box at namecheap.com website. If it is available, you can go ahead and register it.

For domain names, I would suggest you register .com if possible. If you really like the name, but .com is not available, you can try to register the .net version.

Should You Use Your Home Address?

Running a home business does not mean that you must use your home residential address to register for business. When I spoke to some of my friends, some of them are concerned that if they run their business from home, their clients may have a poorer impression of them when they saw their addresses on their name cards. If you are concerned about this issue, then I highly recommend you to register for a virtual office address. There are many virtual office providers out there who will let you use their commercial office address as your own. One example is jje.sg in Singapore.

The advantage of using a virtual office address is that you now have a commercial address that is professional to be printed on your name cards and your clients can even send in their cheques to this address and the virtual office providers will notify you when they receive letters or parcel for you.

A typical cost for a virtual office service is about US$100 per year depending on the country that you are living in.

Back when I was starting out as a Web Developer creating websites for small businesses, I printed my home residential address as my office address on my name cards and very people often commented about the location that I was staying when they saw the address instead of asking me about my business! Hence, I strongly feel that you should use a professional commercial address for your home business.

Must You Have A Separate bank Account for Business?

The answer is yes! First, it makes everything easier to account for. Imagine you have one bank account that is used for your personal and business spending; it will be very difficult to track and recall certain transactions few years down the road. This is especially soul-breaking if you are being audited by the tax authority. So I suggest you form a good habit by creating a separate bank account for your business spending and income.

Different banks do have different packages for corporate accounts. I suggest you shop around for one that suits your needs. Alternatively, you can ask around in your local community to see what the people's recommendations are. You will never go wrong by asking your business friends what banks are they currently using.

How Do You Collect Payment From Your Customers?

With e-commerce getting more and more common, it is now easier to pay online for products and services. And undeniably, you will eventually need to receive payment online from some of your clients.

A good solution is PayPal when you were starting. PayPal allows you to accept payment through credit / debit cards as well as PayPal funds, hence, it is the most popular payment gateway online till date.

All you need to do is to sign up a PayPal business account (at paypal.com) so that you can start to receive money online. Once you have signed up an account, you can generate the payment buttons or links to send to your clients to make payment. After your clients pay you, you can then withdraw the money to your local bank.

Do note that PayPal will charge you transaction fees. You can refer to PayPal website for the transaction fees. In Singapore, I am paying a transaction percentage of 2.9% and $0.50 for every payment I receive.

One misconception consumers have in the market is that they thought they cannot pay by credit or debit card if you send them PayPal payment links. This is not true, and you need to educate your customers. PayPal provides an option for your customers to pay using their cards without creating a PayPal account. This is ideal for almost everyone out there.

Where Can I Get Funding?

I am always grateful that I was born in Singapore because this country is one of the best places in the world to start a business. Most countries do not have grants and schemes to help startups and existing SME (Small and Medium Enterprise) as far as I know.

Under most circumstances, you wouldn't need any funding to start a home business because you will most probably work from home most of the time (saving the office / retail rental cost) and do not have any employees to begin with.

I would still encourage you to take a look at your local government website to search for any available grants or schemes that you can leverage before starting out. In Singapore, most business grants are managed by SPRING (www.spring.gov.sg). If you go to the website, you can find all kinds of grants and assistance available for startups and existing businesses. Although you may not find them useful for you at this point of time, it is always better to be aware of there are such help around.

If you do not have enough savings to start a home business, you can also consider doing a crowd funding campaign.

Crowdfunding means you are enlisting help (in terms of money) from others. For example, starting a home business and you would need help from the public to raise funds for your business. So what is in it for them who help you? You can offer some rewards system for people who contributes to your business funding. For example, if you are starting a web design business and needed money to register a business name, print name cards, marketing materials, etc. You can do a crowd funding campaign, and for people who contributes a certain amount of money, they get a free web design service from you.

You can use the popular crowdfunding portal called Kickstarter.com to start a campaign and start to raise money. If you are living in countries that Kickstarter is not available, then you can try IndieGoGo.

I would expect most people to use their savings to start their home businesses. One more tip; start your home business part-time if you can. By doing so, you will not depend totally on your new business for income as it will take some time to gain traction.

Keeping Proper Book-Keeping Records

When I was starting out as a sole proprietor providing web design services to small businesses, I used to have a

Microsoft excel spreadsheet to help keep track of my expenses and income. This spreadsheet is enough if you just want to use it to monitor your profits or report tax at the end of the year. But if you want to generate your time to date profit / loss statement, you can't...

Hence, I would suggest you use any kind of accounting software to help you manage your expenses and income. Nowadays, there are several cloud-based solutions that you can sign up and use it to keep track of your invoices, expenses, and income. One website is called waveapps. com. You can definitely give it a try!

Whatever the case, I highly recommend you to outsource accounting to a professional if you do not have any accounting background. I have a friend who was an Accountant and he has helped me a lot in terms of accounting and tax report for my company. Working with someone who has the knowledge can greatly reduce the frustrations that you will face and save you time to work on more important things like serving your customers.

Money & Timer Saver Tips

In this section, I will share with you several money and time saver tips that I wish someone were to tell me when I got started! I believe these tips will benefit you greatly even if you already running a home business now.

Affordable & Professional Marketing Materials!

When I just got started in my business, I was so focused on getting the best name card design and the glossiest material for my brochures even before I got my first customer! There is nothing wrong in getting the best design and material for your marketing purpose, but I learn that I should put my focus on getting customers first before I spend money on these shiny objects.

My advice is to strike a balance when you are starting out. On the one hand, you do not want to overspend without having a paying customer first and on the other hand, you do not want to be in a scenario where you also do not have a proper name card!

We are very lucky to live in this time of the world where we can easily get very affordable designers (thanks to the Internet!) online!

If you want to save money and have a professional design for your marketing materials at the same time, then go to fiverr.com. Fiverr.com is a website where a lot of freelancers will help you do a task for $5 or more. For example, I can get someone to design me a name card for $5. I can then pass the design to my local printer to print out the cards for me.

You can also get a logo designer over at Fiverr.com to design a logo for you – at $5!

There are many other services that you can use over at Fiverr.com, but I would suggest that you at least use it to get your name cards and company logo designed there.

This will save you lots of money for marketing later in your business.

These are some tips for you when you are choosing a freelancer over at Fiverr.com. First, sort the results according to the highest rating. Second, go through each freelancer and see how many reviews they have. Normally I will go with the one with a very high number of reviews (in the range of thousands). Next, browse through the reviews written by the previous buyers and see if there is any negative experience. If no, you can safely pay that person for the job.

Virtual Office Services

Perhaps one not-so-good thing about working from home is the impression that you give to your potential customers. Some customers will think that you are just starting out when they see that your name card shows your residential address. A solution to this concern is to register for a virtual office address that you can use for your business.

A virtual office address service is not expensive as I am only paying about SG$10 per month for my virtual office address in Singapore.

Having a virtual office address allows you not only to use it as your business address, but also you can ask your customers to send their cheques to this address. The virtual office will collect the letters for you daily and notify you on a daily basis.

Frankly, I find that a virtual office service is a great help to us who work from home. Without having to pay for expensive rental in commercial buildings, now you can use an address that has a higher perceived value.

When you are shopping around for virtual office service, take note of the address where they are located. In Singapore, there are many such providers and they all located at different areas in the country. Choose a business district where it is not so far from where you stay because you will need to travel to collect letters once a while. Also, some virtual office service providers also have conference or meeting rooms for you to rent and use in times of need. So consider your option carefully before you commit to one because changing the virtual office address also means that you need to change your address on your name card in future.

Accounting & Book-keeping!

Frankly, I know nothing about accounting and this area of the business is where I dislike it the most! But running a home business also means that you must know everything so you can manage it. You may not need to do it yourself, but you need to know what is going on.

As a home business owner, you need to keep proper accounting records such as your business expense, invoices, income, receipts. Some of you may think that using an excel spreadsheet is enough, but when your business starts to grow, and you start to have someone working for you, you will find that it is a headache maintaining all your records in excel format. I highly suggest you use an accounting software to keep your records from the start so that when your business grows, it is much easier to scale up.

My best suggestion is to make friends with people who have accounting knowledge before you start a business. What I did when I incorporate my company is that I ask one of my business friends to help me to the registration, and from there on, he now helps me to do our annual AGM (Annual General Meeting), tax filing and at times when we have some questions on accounting, we will always check with him (of course, we pay for his services annually).

I find that it is always better to work with an expert especially in the area that you don't like to do. This will give you the maximum leverage in business, and you can invest that extra time into your business whether it is marketing or serving customers.

Website Development and Design!

One of the marketing materials that you need when you run a home business is a professional website to showcase your products or services. After I met someone new, I will always go check out their website (if I am interested in what they do) at my own time.

It is very common for potential customers to search for your services online nowadays. Hence, you must have a professional website to give a good first impression to people who visited your website.

Depending on the type of websites that you want to create, web design companies may charge you anywhere from US$1,000 (informational website) to US$3,500 (e-commerce website). If you do not have the budget, you may want to learn and create a website on your own.

Today, we are fortunate that not only programmers can create websites. With technology like WordPress being invented, you are now able to create a website without any programming knowledge. There are a lot of affordable online courses that you can take to learn how to create a website for your business. Udemy is one of the most popular platforms online that has a lot of courses including website creation that you can sign up. Once you get Udemy, you can search for 'WordPress course' as it is easier to learn compared to other website creation courses.

Here I want to share with you my experiences with other business friends as these experiences may benefit you in the long run. When I was conducting website training courses, there are several business owners come and attend because their web developers are charging them a huge sum to revamp and maintain their websites. These business owners think that it is time to take control of their websites and not to be "taken advantage" of when they need help in their website improvements.

The disadvantages of having someone taking care of your website is that you must have the budget and that web developing company may disappear or be acquired by someone else.

If you were to learn and create the website yourself, there are disadvantages as well. You need to invest some time to learn especially in the beginning. But once you gained the momentum, this skill stays with you forever. The best thing is, you can update your website anytime you want without the need to pay a maintenance fee.

If you still think that it would be too time-consuming to learn and create the website yourself, then this is my best advice I will give you: **get someone to create your website in WordPress then ask that person to teach you how to maintain it**.

This is sort of the best of both worlds because it eliminates the time for you to learn to create a website from scratch. Honestly, what gives the most frustrations to business owners when they are learning to create a website is the beginning when they are starting to learn, install and configure the site. Once you outsource this part and get it done by someone else, you only need to learn how to update your website from there. This will save you a lot of money in the long run.

Marketing Strategy!

When I first got started in my business, I did not have any experience in marketing. In fact, I don't even know what is marketing… I learn the hard way by looking at what others are doing and try out myself. After all these years of learning from my own and others' mistakes, I have compiled the most effective ways (the things I am doing now) to generate my business. In the following pages, you will learn the top 20% of the things I do to generate 80% of my customers.

There are three marketing channels that I highly encourage everyone to work hard and implement them:

1) Word Of Mouth

2) Strategic Partnership

3) Speaking

If you ask any successful businessmen on what is their most effective channel to get customers, most of them will tell you word-of-mouth. Word of mouth is easy for new Entrepreneurs who are starting out to understand but implementing it is another thing. I will do my best to simplify this concept into actionable steps in the following.

First, if you are serious in learning to benefit from word of mouth marketing, I highly recommend you to read the book *"The Referral Engine: Teaching Your Business to Market Itself"* by John Jantsch. This is the best book I have read so far on the topic of word of mouth.

The advantage of word of mouth is that you don't need to allocate any marketing budget like advertising. People get to know of your services mainly because of your existing customers helping you to spread the words for you.

To get the word of mouth effect, you first have to acknowledge that you will not get the results fast. It often takes years to see the results of word of mouth. Hence, you need to be patience, and while you are waiting for the word of mouth to get you most of your business, you need to work on other channels concurrently.

The following are three tips I have for you to have the word of mouth effect for your business:

Word-Of-Mouth

Exceed expectation. If you are active in social media, you will notice sometimes your friends will share some exceptionally good services by some cafes or restaurants. I still remember that one of my friends shared that he accidentally spilled his fries and drinks in a Macdonald outlet and the staff quickly come forward and ask if my friend is alright. Immediately after, the staff came up to him with another drink and fries freshly prepared for my friend. This is an example of one of the exceptional good services.

Nowadays, people like to shop online and have the things shipped to their houses. One of the examples is that some online stores surprised their customers by upgrading their shipping option without letting the customers know. Hence, the items arrived much faster without the customers expecting them!

In your business when serving your customers, think of ways that you can delight your customers. One helpful way is to look at different industries at how they delight their customers. Use those as a reference and think creativity how you can delight your customers or even prospects.

Do not focus on referral fee to generate word of mouth. This is a very practical advice that I would like you to bear in mind at all times. I was a member of the Business Network International (BNI) some years back. I can still remember that in my chapter (a group of business owners), there was this member who does land banking. He does not have many referrals for his area of investment and hence, he came up with incentives to reward his business friends if they refer their friends to him.

The results are pathetic. For many months, referrals still didn't come in for him. He eventually left the chapter. The lesson I want to share here is that money is not the main factor that people refer their friends. BNI has once done a study with its thousands of members and found out that the number one reason why people recommend their friends to you is the character and integrity of the Entrepreneur. If you always do what you say and delight customers with exceptional value, people are going to refer more businesses to you regardless if you have any referral fee program.

If there is one thing that you can take away from this section, remember; instead of focusing your energy to come up with a referral fee structure, invest your energy into providing great value to your customers!

Always ask how your customers came to know about you. I always ask people who contacted me about my services how they got to know about me. You must make this a habit because this is the only accurate way to find out how effective is your marketing effort. You will be surprised that some people mentioned sources that you will never think of!

Most of the time, they will mention an existing client of mine and tell me that they were referred by them. Now, upon knowing that person's name, you must take note and send him/her a thank-you card! If for whatever reason you don't want to send a card, make sure you at least make a call and thank them personally!

I find that it is important to acknowledge the person who keeps on referring businesses to you. There are two reasons for this.

First, people sometimes will refer their friends who you may not want to serve (wrong target market). So this is a good time to feedback and let them know that their referrals are not exactly the type of businesses you are looking for. This is the perfect time to educate your friend because you wouldn't want this to repeat again. Most new business owners do nothing about this, and it wasted a possible good source of referral!

Second, everyone wants to feel important and appreciated. When someone kept referring you your ideal businesses but didn't always hear anything from you, they will eventually stop referring you if you did not acknowledge them. The best thing to do is to thank your referral source personally if you can. The second best method is to send them a personally written card. The next best way is to give them a call and at least tell them that these are the clients you are looking for!

Strategic Partners

It is good to have your clients talking about you, but this method can be slow to get clients especially in the beginning. In the beginning, you would need things to get moving faster so that you can keep up the momentum.

A faster way to get clients without your active time is through strategic partnership. This means that you work with someone who also serves your target market and cross refer clients to one another.

Let me share with you my story on this case.

Three months into starting my business back in 2008, I did not manage to find one single client myself. I was near to the point where I going to call my ex-employer and went back to 9-to-5 job. One day, my friend introduced me to one of his friends who is the manager of a popular company in Singapore providing business registration services. This manager gets to know what I was doing at that time (which is developing websites) and suggests we can work together because every day he will have clients wanting to register a new business and perhaps they also need a website.

That simple meetup changed my life totally, and I was receiving calls every day asking me to do websites for them. This is what I called a perfect partnership!

I want you to think of who are the people also serving your target market so that you can start to network and meet up with them even before you start your business. For example, if you are a graphics designer who serves the local small businesses community, you want to work with professions who also serve the small businesses, like Printers, Marketing Consultants, and Accountancy firms.

My best suggestion in this section is never give up and always look for the ideal partnership until you found one that injects abundance into your business! Attend networking events and always educating your friends what you are doing. Given some time, good things will come your way if you persist!

Speaking Opportunities

Another excellent way of marketing your business is to get in front a group of people and share what you know. When I first started my business, I am fearful of speaking, and I'm always anxious especially when I know I am the next speaker!

Slowly, I realize that this is an important aspect of a profitable business. As a home business owner (or any business owner), you must be ready to share what you do and your knowledge to anyone. This will create the leverage that you can't find in providing services or selling products to one person at a time.

To illustrate the power of speaking, let me share with you my story. After providing website development services for small businesses for a few years, I figured that I might prefer teaching them how to create a website rather than creating for them. Hence, I converted my business model to training and conducting workshops. Every month, I will run classes of about 10 to 20 participants coming to learn website creation. And out of these 10 plus participants, there will always be 1 or 2 persons coming up to me after the class asking me if I can create websites for their companies!

I realize that by speaking or training, some people will begin to trust you and even ask you to help them. This is the leverage I like. Conducting a class and still able to provide services to a selected group of clients. To me, this is the best of both worlds!

Even when I was a guest speaker in other events, there are always people coming up to me after my talk to ask me if I can help them create websites. There are also countless of cases where people called me months after my talk!

I hope that you see the benefit of speaking and most important, getting the leverage!

One of the best ways to get such speaking opportunities is to get to know some event organisers. I find that most event organisers are looking for guest speakers at some point of the time. Hence, getting to know them will increase the chance they ask you to speak. One of the things I do is I tend to do is to arrive very early for networking events to get a chance to speak to the organizer before the event starts and ask if there is anything I can help.

There are several advantages for arriving very early. First, you will be one of the first people to meet the organizer so that the organizer will remember you better. Second, by helping out in the event, you will not feel as tense especially if you are very new to networking!

If you think you are an introvert and by any chance, you live in Singapore, then I want to recommend that you attend the Networking for Introverts community meetup organized by Mr Mervin Yeo. I find that Mervin's events are set up to help and guide people who are new in networking especially introverts. You can search for "Introverts Network, Singapore" inside facebook and join the closed group first and get to know the members there.

I hope that I have convinced you that speaking is one of the best ways to get your business known by more people in a very cost effective way. I also understand that most people do not like (fear, anxiety, etc.) to speak in front of a group especially if you have not done this before. I want to share with you an effective way to reduce your fear and anxiety when you speak. The keyword is – Preparation.

To me, anxiety and fear will be greatly reduced if I am well prepared for a talk and especially when I have prepared some interesting stories to share with the audience! Hence, you must be 100% prepared for the talk and rehearse as many times as you can especially one to two days before the event, even though your speaking time is one or two minutes!

I find that many people are not prepared to share what they do and know when they are asked to do so. As a home business owner, you must always be ready to tell people what you do or know. As such, I suggest you have different lengths of speech like one, five and thirty minute for different occasions!

Another good way to have speaking opportunities is to organize your own talks! What you can do to start off is to gather a few friends of your and host a small meetup and facilitate the session to share each of your expertise and explore ways to help out one another. This is a very common way to start among a group of new business owners.

At the end of the day, I hope you are more prepared the next time people ask you to share what you do. Remember, speaking is one of the best leverage any business owners can get!

Success Marketing Blueprint

In this chapter, I want to share with you a proven way to start and run a profitable home business - using my "Success Marketing Blueprint". If you have not started any business before, you may be overwhelmed by the term "Marketing Plan". If so, no worries as I will step you through a simple but yet effective plan to generate businesses for you.

1 - Your Core Marketing Message

The first step in this blueprint is to develop your core marketing message. The reason for doing so is to help you reduce time and resources selling to people who will not buy from you no matter how hard you sell.

This exercise will also help you identify your target market and what are they really **buying** from you. Many business owners nowadays don't even know who are their target market after several years in business, don't make this mistake!

The core marketing template is in this format:

I help _____ (Target Market) to _____ (what people buy) by _____ (solving their problems)!

Target Market

First, let's identify who are your target market. In other words, who are the ideal customers that you want to serve? Take, for example, if you are running an accounting firm and you want to help small businesses who have 5 or fewer employees to manage their accounts, then your target market is small business owners with less than 5 employees.

If you are an image consultant and you want to help young entrepreneurs to improve their first impression when they meet their clients, then your target market will be young entrepreneurs who just started their businesses.

You can have more than one target market, and it won't be a problem, but you need to identify your main target market. I suggest that you don't have more than three target market because that will dilute your core marketing message.

One common mistake people make is that they tend to make their target market very broad and cover a lot of people. For example, a Taichi Instructor may identify all people above 50 years old as his/her target market. This often will not lead to an effective marketing message. Instead, the TaiChi Instructor should break it down further, for example, people above 50 years old with arthritis issue.

Once you have identified your target market, you need to do some simple research to see if your target market is too small. This step is important because you wouldn't want to serve a small market, especially if there are other professions doing what you are going to do. You can do a simple research online using the Google Keyword Planner tool to find out how many people are searching for your product or services online every month. I suggest a minimum of 3,000 monthly searches for you to start your home business.

What People Really Buying

The next thing to look into is to ask yourself this question "What people are really buying from you?" For someone who walks into a shop selling glasses, do you think that person wants to really buy a spectacle? My answer is no; he wants a better vision. Another example, people who buy locks for their houses do not just want the lock, they want the security that the lock creates for them!

Until you know the real reason why people wants to buy your solution, you will be having a hard time designing your marketing materials to achieve the results you want.

Solving their problems

The answer to the third blank is more straight-forward. If you help people to prevent hair loss and grow more hairs naturally, then this is the exact solution.

Now with all the three answers, you can piece them together to form your core marketing message. The following is an example for a hair treatment specialist who specialize in preventing and helping people to grow hair naturally.

I help **stressful working professionals** *(Target Market) to* **increase confidence, gain self-esteem** *(what people buy) by* **preventing hair loss and growing more hair naturally** *(solving their problems)!*

2- Create your first premium!

Once you have your core marketing message developed, you are now a great step ahead of your competitors. Your next task is to create a freemium as a lead magnet to attract customers to you.

A Freemium is something (of great value) that you give away to achieve the following two points:

1. Show your expertise in what you do.

2. Serve as a lead magnet for someone to give you the permission to follow up.

Let me give you an example, I have a good friend who is in accountancy business. He often meet up with his prospects and share with them what he does. At the end of the session, he will not ask for business (yet!) but to give them a template that they can use for free to keep track of their business activities. On first thought, you may think that no one will ever come back to him for business if he keeps giving his template away, right? But that's not the case, people are going back to him because they find that they don't want to waste their time recording in that template and rather have someone helps them to manage the accounts and also book-keeping.

The above example is a perfect scenario of showing how a giver's mentality can benefit by serving others first. In today's fast moving marketplace, everyone is looking to close a sale as quickly as possible then move on. The more people do this, the more you need to do the opposite. Hence, strategizing your freemium is very important before you head out and tell people about your services or products!

There are a few common types of freemium you can create:

1. **Free Trial** – Free trial commonly applies to software or tools that you have developed. It means that you give a free trial of 30 days for someone to try out your product and if that person likes it, he / she will purchase from there. This freemium work best for businesses who has a certain leverage. Software is a great example of this type of freemium. I know a friend whose name is Irwin, he runs a popular tuition business in Singapore, and he gave free trials for people to attend his tuition class when he first started his business. This model also works for him especially when not all his class is fully seated. Thus, by increasing the number of students, it does not increase the overheads directly.

2. **Free Instructional Videos** – Another very common type of freemium is giving away instructional

videos in exchange of your potential customers' contact information such as email addresses. This approach is commonly practiced in the Internet marketing arena where people teaches how to create websites or show how to generate traffic for certain products. If you are in a service-based business, then this will be a method for you to consider. I used to give away free videos to introduce different types of online businesses to increase my mailing list subscription rate before I recommend them the various in-depth training courses.

3. **Free Guide / Checklist** – Free guide can be instructional document or PDF that teaches someone to do something. You can also compile a checklist and use that as a freemium. Take for example if you are an Accountant, you can create a checklist for small business owners to check what they need to submit their annual returns. Checklist can be useful for tasks that are not commonly performed by someone, but it is important not to miss out any steps.

4. **Free Chapters of Your Book** – If you are a published Author, you can give away the first chapter of your book to encourage subscription to your mailing list. The thing about this type of freemium is that not many business owners are Authors themselves, but if you are, this is a good way to position yourself and also increase your subscribers to keep them updated. You do not need to be an Author of a hardcopy book in order to do this, you can simply be an eBook writer also. Just make sure you extract the interesting chapter(s) out of your book to keep

the readers engaged and want to come back to you for more!

5. **Discount Coupons** – This type of freemium is very commonly practiced in the e-commerce industry. Most e-commerce shop owner uses discounts to attract visitors to become their customers. You can also use this tactic to get your first sale from your website visitors. For example, you can give away a 25% discount coupon if they become your subscribers and they can use the discount coupon within the next 30 days!

At the end of the day, your freemium will help you to get subscribers to your mailing list so that you can keep them updated in future. Many business owners create automated emails to be sent to their mailing list especially in the first 30 days when someone becomes their subscribers. This is a very effective way to turn your subscribers into customers because you are using an educational-based approach. Once people perceive you as the domain expert, they are more likely to buy from you.

3- Gather Testimonials

Once you have prepared your freemium, you must first gather testimonials before you start offering your services in the marketplace. You may ask how to have testimonials before you sell? The answer is simple – provide a service to someone in exchange for a testimonial!

When I first got started, no one wants to get me to design websites for them because I have no portfolio and no one on Earth wants to be the first customer of a new business, trust me! Hence, your objective in this third step is to provide your service to someone you know or a charitable organization without any fee but in exchange of a testimonial. This will help you build up your portfolio and also gather stories to share with your potential customers in future. While I'm at this, stories are an effective way to connect with your prospects and make them believe that you are the best candidate to help them.

Your target in this phase is to serve and collect at least 10 testimonials so that you have enough stories and portfolio to share whenever you meet someone. One of the best ways to start is to approach your friends to kick start the process.

4- Real Business Starts!

Once you have collected the 10 testimonials, put them up on your website, social media profiles such as LinkedIn. This will help you to attract other people who are interested in engaging your services.

Selling will be much easier with the stories and testimonials you have collected. Many times I find that sharing my other customers' stories (before and after they engaged my services) with prospects increase the conversion rate. This involves practicing, hence, always be ready to share stories that is relevant to the current prospects that you are talking to.

These four steps are important, and I urge you to follow them if you want to start and run a profitable business without repeating the mistakes I have made years ago.

Now that you know my marketing blueprint, it is time for me to share with you some of the costly mistakes you must avoid when you start a business!

SEVEN EXPENSIVE MISTAKES TO AVOID!

1. Start Networking Too Late!

This is one of the most commonly made mistakes especially if you are new to business. Many people would wait until they registered and started their business then start attending networking events. I often suggest my friends who are keen to start a business to start attending networking events soon because it takes time for people you meet to trust and like you before any business transactions happened.

When I ask my friends to start attending networking events, one of the most common rejections they will say is they don't know what to say if people were to ask them what they do. I understand this concern and would like to share this tip with you. If you are still working on your full-time job but wanting to start a business soon, you can simply tell people that you are planning to start a business soon in which area. You will be surprised that there are so many people out there who is very supportive and they may even introduce you to their contacts to help you launch your business faster!

I just want to share with you that it takes time to build relationships for business transactions to happen. Don't ever wait until you start your business officially then go for networking, it would be too late!

There are many networking events available in the country, you can visit meetup.com and search for a relevant event that you can attend. Choose something that relates to business or professional meetups because these categories are more relevant to your future business development.

2. Chasing After Every Single Opportunity!

The second common mistake is to chase after every business opportunity when they arise!

I kid you not. I have been in business since 2008, and ever since then, I have seen many Entrepreneurs changing what they do every time I meet them in networking events. For example, one day I met this person named Max and he was selling air purifiers but several months later, I met Max in another event and he told me that now he is a grant consultant as Government is introducing several grants for the small businesses. Then another few months passed and I met him somewhere now he told me he is a property agent because the property market is recovering...

I wanted to share with you the above encounter because there are many people out there who is like Max. I do not want you to be like Max because people will not think of Max if they needed a real estate agent (most people will think of someone they know who have done something for quite some time rather than just beginning). If you start a business with the only aim is money, then high chance you will end up like Max. But if you started a business with the aim to serve a gap in the market and make life easier for your customers, then I would say you are in for an excellent ride!

There are many temptations when you are in the business world, know what you want before you step out there!

3. **Rejecting Speaking Opportunities!**

The third mistake you must avoid is to reject any speaking opportunity!

I know that public speaking is not easy for most people, but as a business owner, you must learn to share your experiences and what you do readily. If you reject a speaking opportunity, you are missing a great platform to leverage your time. Speaking is one of the most effective methods to expose your business to many people in a time.

If you have fears in public speaking, you can start by arranging a small event or meetup and be the host to introduce speakers. As time passes, you will get more comfortable speaking in front of a group, and once you build that confidence in you, you can start to approach event organizers and share with them your speaking topics.

One of the tips of how I attract speaking opportunities is to get to know event organizers whenever you attend an event. Do your best to be early and get to know the host if you can, and if it is a small event, you can even offer your help. Event organizers often need help in finding guest speakers so if you increase your visibility by offering your help and getting to know the host, eventually you will be asked to share your topic.

Learning how to leverage is very important to build a successful business. Speaking is an excellent way to leverage without any investment on your part. Become a speaker who regularly speaks, and you will find people coming to you wanting to find out more!

4. **Buy First, Sell Later!**

Buy first, sell later has always been the traditional business model since the beginning of time. If you want to set up a store in a shopping mall, you would have to pay for the rental and buy the inventory before you even start selling. This has always been the case... until now.

Instead of buying first and selling later, I want you to think of **Sell First, Buy Later**! If you master this concept, you will never lose money in business.

With the invention of Internet, now we are able to sell first then buy later. Let me give you an example. Years ago, I met up with one of my e-commerce students somewhere on the streets, and I asked her how she is doing. She said she is doing great, she is now selling things online. I was happy for her and asked her what she sells. She replies that she sells things from Daiso (which is a $2 shop in Singapore) and resell them for higher price online! I was amazed at the idea and told her that she got a winner as her investment per product is only $2. She replies saying that no, her investment is zero. She then continued saying that when she goes to that store, she would only take pictures of the products then put online. Only when someone pays her online, then she will go and buy then ship over.

What a brilliant idea!

The reason I want to share with you the above story is because with the invention of Internet, now anyone can sell first then buy later. That day I was shopping online for books and two days after I made payment, the online bookstore refunded my money saying that there is no stock for the books I ordered. I can assure you that there are many online stores practice the concept of sell first, buy later. They don't have the stock themselves too! It is only after they received the money, then they go to the source and buy.

Next time before you invest something in your business, always think of how you can sell first then buy later. Practice creativity and think differently – this is the skill that you need to be a successful business owner. Once you successfully changed your mindset, you will see there are so many opportunities around us!

5. Quitting Your Full-Time Job Too Soon!

The next mistake that I want you to avoid is quitting your job too soon. I myself made that mistake back in 2008 when I think I should be able to make a living with my newly acquired skills. What a foolish thought!

I want you to start part-time first instead of full-time because that process will help you learn many skills you need in business. For example, you will need to learn how to sell, and if you still have a full-time job, it won't put stresses on you especially if you have a family to support.

The main purpose of starting part-time is to proof that your concept works and your business can generate income while you do it at the side. You will be surprised that it will take a while for your business to be profitable and as long as you do it part-time while having a steady full-time income, you can take your time to learn the ropes.

I suggest that you only quit your job if you have generated the same level of income from your part-time business as compared to your full-time job. You may think that it is difficult, but it is possible. In order to achieve that, you must forget about you doing the operations and think scaling the business through leveraging. If there is one important skill you must learn in business, I would say that is leverage.

6. Not Asking For Referrals!

Another common mistake most new business owners make is they don't ask for referrals from their customers. I don't know if it is my introvert nature that I learn this the hard way... When I first started my business, I thought that if my service is good, people will refer my services to their friends. Well, I only got the first part of the equation correct. Most people will refer only if you ask them to.

Most people are busy with their lives, so they don't actively go around sharing with others about your business unless there is a chance and they remembered you. So if you are just going to wait for others to refer businesses to you, you will have to wait for a long while!

My suggestion is to at least let your friends, prospects, and customers know that you rely a lot on referrals. One of the best timings to let your customers know is when you have completed the services for them. Tell them that you are very happy to serve them and would be glad to serve their friends too especially if they have the same profile.

Some companies train their staff to deliberately ask the clients to write down three friends who they can call and follow-up. I personally do not like this technique as it comes across too hard-selling. You may adopt this practice if you find that it is ok but for me, I prefer something more subtle while not totally passive and wait for things to happen.

Asking for referrals is also a skill, you need to craft your questions carefully. I would suggest that you read up more about this topic especially the book written by John Jantsch *"The Referral Engine: Teaching Your Business To Market Itself!"*.

Keep practicing the art of asking, and I am sure it will become second nature for you!

7. **Not Leveraging!**

Although this is the last of the seven mistakes I have for you but this does not mean that this is the least damaging, in fact, this mistake is one of the costly ones as it may cost your most valuable asset – time.

Many new business owners do not understand the power of leverage and want to do everything themselves. This is a very common thinking, and this is the reason why so many businesses fail!

In order to create a profitable business and having the time for yourself and your family, you must master the leverage formula. Think of how you can best leverage the resources around you so that your business can run without your active involvement.

There are two areas you can leverage. First is technology. Take, for example, I first started teaching in a classroom, and my income would stop when I stop teaching. But since 2014, I started to record all my training into videos so anyone can just come online and watch my recorded tutorials anytime they want without me teaching live. In a short two years, I enrolled more than 20,000 students online which I may not be possible to achieve this number by doing offline in a classroom setting!

Another way you can leverage using technology is email. One of my favorite online tools is called GetResponse. It is an email marketing platform that allows me to put a sign-up box in my website so that my visitors can sign up and receive a freebie. Once someone signs up, they will start to receive educational and promotional emails once a while. All these emails are pre-written by me and saved into Get-Response so that the system can send them out for me.

Especially if you are working from home and most likely starting your business alone or with another person, do your best to think how you can best leverage technology and do things for you instead of your own active time.

Another very common aspect of leverage is people. For big corporations, they have the power of leverage because there are so many people working for the same company and as long as the people generate more money than they are getting paid, the corporation will be profitable. Similarly, you need to get someone to do what you do in terms of operation so that you can focus on growing your business. Of course, for that to happen, you must be able to generate businesses first.

For example, if I am a web designer and I create websites for other businesses. If I managed to partner with someone or implemented a marketing plan that brings me more deals that I can manage alone, I must get someone to do the things I do so that I can free up my time to grow the business. So in this case, you can hire someone to design website for you, or do the closing of deals, or both. At the end of the day, you must first develop a system for marketing and bringing in deals more than you can manage than you can apply this aspect of leverage.

You may find it difficult to remember all these 7 mistakes all at once so I want to suggest that you come back to this section of the book as often as you can remember. I can assure you that if you come back to this section again after you started your business for some time, you will be able to relate even better with what I have shared above.

The 3Cs To Have A Profitable Home Business!

In Singapore, I conduct workshops periodically to teach people how to start a profitable home business, and I always share my 3C formula that the participants must remember for them to create a profitable business. I am going to share with you this 3C formula and please take this section seriously because all (yes, ALL) profitable home business must have these 3Cs.

First C - **Contacts**

Contacts are the pre-requisite for a profitable business, but in this case, I don't mean the all the contacts you have in your address book. I mean qualified contacts that will help you in your business! Read on...

There are two types of contact that you must establish before you start your business. The first group is your target market, the second is professions who serve your target market. Again, never wait until you started a business then go and establish and build relationships, always start getting to know people before you start your business.

Let me share about the target market group first. Before you start a business, you must identify who are your target market, for example, if you are a Web Designer, your target market can be people who just registered their businesses and needed a website. Or your target market can be long time businesses who needed to upgrade their websites. Both are possible targets, but you need to identify who you want to serve first.

Once you identified your target market, you need to think of where and how to get to know these people. For example, if you are targeting newly married couples for your services, you need to know where can you find them and start to get to know as many of them as possible. You can search for meetup groups and online forums where your target market hangs out then start to network there.

The other group is profession who serve your target market. For example, if your target market is new business owners, identify who are also serving these people. Professions who serve new business owners can be named card printers, logo designers, web hosting providers and accountants. Once you identify all the possible professions, start to get to know these people to discuss collaboration after building the relationships.

The best advice for you is not to blindly attend networking events and invest time in people who do not fall into the above two groups of people. Networking can be draining especially if you are an Introvert like me, hence, spend your time wisely. Time is precious when you are running your own business!

Second C - **Customers**

The second C stands for customers. Having good and qualified contacts without turning them into customers is pointless. The key here is to turn your target market into customers and professions who served your target market into partners.

Many people called the process of turning contacts into customers as selling. If you think like that, it would be very difficult for you to turn them into customers. Selling is tough, and for most people like us, we are not trained for sales, and furthermore, I believe not many people out there like to do sales.

I like to call this conversion process as education instead of selling. For the past few years, I figured out that the main reason why people don't buy from me is not because of the price, or I am not good in what I do. **It is because that I didn't clearly educate my prospects what value I can add to their lives**. Thus, I want you to remember by heart that to convert your contacts into customers, you need to constantly educate them what value you add and have added to your customers. When your contacts see the value that they will be having from you, they will come to you and ask you for your service.

I have a friend who provides accountancy services for businesses. He always shares generously about what he knows to anyone he meets even though they could be potential clients for him. His generosity is what makes him likable and trustable by many who eventually engage him for his services. Thus, I highly encourage you to position yourself as an educator than a sales professional.

This process also takes a while so don't expect to see results quickly. People take time to find out if they trust someone enough to do business with them so do not rush things over.

Third C - **Cash**

The third C is cash. No businesses are profitable if there are no paying customers. Once you turn contacts into customers, you start to collect cash so that your business can survive and thrive.

This third C also means that you must be very good in controlling the cash flow of your business. Many new business owners tend to spend money on things that often unnecessary in the beginning like fanciful name cards and marketing materials. What you need in the beginning is to invest as little as you can but still achieve the results.

You need to keep thinking how you can sell first, and buy later. Because if you can achieve what you want without spending money first, then your business can go far. For example, if you want to rent a place to do an educational seminar and also share your services with more people, you can create an online registration form to accept payment first before you rent a place for event. Some people would pay for a place first then do the marketing, this is not a wise approach as compared to collecting the money first so that you make sure you don't make a loss conducting seminar.

All in all, these 3 Cs will help you start a profitable business in any economy. Remember them well, and they will serve you in the coming many years of Entrepreneurship!

Six Timeless Secrets For A Successful Home Business!

In this section, you will learn eight secrets I have for you through these years of running my business and learning from other experienced business owners. Are you ready? Here we go!

Don't Do It Just For Money!

Never start a business just because of money. If you start a business just because of money, you will find yourself giving up before you know it! Especially when you are faced with challenges along the way. Trust me, challenges are here to come and hence, you need stronger reasons to stay in this game longer to run a profitable business!

Instead of putting focus on money, you should shift your focus to fill a gap in the current market. Is there any gap in the current market that no one is serving? Or a problem that frustrates you but no one is solving? These are opportunities for you to bridge the gap and start a meaningful business to serve and add real value to people.

I have seen too many people started their businesses just for money and end up switching businesses because they didn't persist enough when problems crop up.

When you start a business filling a gap and truly wants to help your customers, you will think of ways to make your services better along the way. You will also won't be afraid of competitors because you know that you will have an edge over your competitors when you serve from your heart.

Before I end this section, remember that never use the lowest price to be the edge of your business, price war is not a good strategy for business and the entire marketplace.

Don't Just Be Better, Be Different!

One of the stories that I always share with my friends is when I started teaching WordPress many years ago, that time, I was the only WordPress Trainer in Singapore and when you google for 'WordPress course', you will see my course schedule listed on first page. As time goes by, more and more WordPress trainers emerge and started to conduct classes at a cheaper rate than mine.

One day, I sat down and thought what can I do to be different (instead of just lowering my price then do what most Trainers did). I thought of a great idea in that few days – this is, to conduct WordPress class for free! Yes, you didn't hear me wrong, I didn't charge a single cent for my class, but instead, all the participants who join my class have to sign up my hosting plans in order to join for free. This new business model improved the sign ups for my WordPress class because now participants don't need to pay anything just the hosting fee for their websites. This business model also allows me to make recurring income (yearly hosting fees) than compared to the one-time training fees.

The reason I share with you this story is because if you want to help your customers, you will have that creativity to be different than your competitors.

Creativity is the most important skill for any Entrepreneurs if you ask me. If you are creative, you will never have to fear of any competitors because the most they can do is to copy you, which the best they can do is catching up.

I believe everyone can be creative, and be different. Stop following what others are doing and create your own unique style (with added value) and eventually people will want to follow you because of you. Not because of the low price or other marketing gimmicks.

Be A Keen Learner, Absorb, and Implement Fast!

One of the best tips I have ever learnt from my business mentors is keep learning and implement immediately what you learn whether it is in books, live seminar or on-line learning.

I know some of my friends who keep attending seminars and buying books to read and learn from the experts, but after gaining the knowledge, they move on to the next expert and learn instead of reflecting what they can implement from their learning. One of my strengths is that I always summarize one thing (minimally) that I can do differently after reading a book or attending an event. This has helped me grow so much in terms of business because I try different things and in my domain of expertise where I continue to explore new ways to help my customers.

Both implementation and learning are important here if you keep learning without stopping and reflect, it is equivalent to no learning in the first place. If you keep doing but didn't allocate time to learn new things, your business will eventually stagnate and decline. Learn to implement something after a learning session, this way, you will be on your way to constant improvements.

When reading a new book, my aim is to at least take away one thing that I can implement in my daily life or work. That would mean that I have ROI (Returns On Investment) the whole book! Many people read a book taking down notes on almost everything but eventually get overwhelmed because we as humans are not designed to adapt many new habits at one time. Instead, we work better by adapting slowly, making one new habit at a time.

Give Your Business Enough Time To Grow!

Most people quit just before they were about to see the fruits of their hard work. There is a saying that sometimes success belongs to those that hang on the longest. In today's fast moving marketplace, people tend to think and act first. This may not be a good thing when it comes to a very important decision like quitting.

From these years of experiences, I saw that too many people give up too soon. Especially new business owners when they see that their sales are not coming in, one of the first things that they thought of is maybe this business is not for them. I would say that just merely a few months is not enough to assess if a business if worth quitting. Typically, it takes a year or two to see the returns of your effort, hence, be prepared to invest and work hard (and smart) in the first few years without expecting huge returns in the beginning. Time is essential in this success formula when you want to be successful in business.

I want to share with you the story of the Chinese bamboo.

> I believe that nature has a way of teaching us time-less lessons about life and I want to share with you the story of the Chinese bamboo today.
>
> Now, try imagining yourself growing a bamboo plant. After carefully planting the seed in the soil, you water and care for it every day.
>
> 10 days passed, but there is no sign of growth. You continue to water it for another 3 weeks. Still, nothing seems to be growing.
>
> 2 months later, you look at the soil... in disbelief. There is still *nothing*.
>
> Many people would have given up by now. It's been 2 months! It's easy to think 'the seed must have died' or 'why should I be wasting my time? It's not working.'
>
> But what about you? Will you plan to give up now?
>
> In fact, you have literally nothing to show for in the first, second or even the third year... In the fourth year, the soil is *still* barren.
>
> Four long years of hard work – has it all gone down the drain? Hold on. Look what happens...

In the fifth year, not only does your bamboo plant sprout from the ground, it shoots up to *ninety* feet tall in six weeks!

Just imagine, what would it be if you had given up?

You would never have gotten the chance to see how amazing your little bamboo seed *can* become.

The key lesson to take away here is the importance of patience, persistence, and consistency.

KC Tan

Never Stop Networking

I see that many business owners stopped networking after they have a consistent stream of customers going to them. On the surface, it is easy to see that networking takes up time and you might be better off focusing on serving your customers instead of networking. But from my experiences, every time I stopped doing networking, my streams of customers or referrals will stop after a while.

I slowly learned that networking is not a temporary activity, but it is a habit that all business owners must adapt and do it regularly, even if it is once a month. There are a lot of benefits when it comes to networking. First, it will help you to stay in touch with the local business community on the latest and upcoming trends. For example, in Singapore, our government frequently assist small businesses with grants so staying in touch with the community allow me to hear and learn from other business owners about the latest grant that we can use for ourselves.

Another big advantage of networking is it will train you how to present yourself. The first impression still counts a big deal! Hence, you need to be aware of how you present yourself especially at times when you represent your business. By interacting with others, sometimes you will also see yourself in them. And this gives you a new perspective on how you can better present yourself.

To me, the biggest advantage after attending all these years of networking events is to meet people whom I can collaborate with. I always share my story in my live workshop where you only need to find one star partner and it will help you to breakthrough and achieve the next level. In the early years when I started my business, I managed to find a partner who referred me 80% of my clients. This partner generated so many sales for me that I do not have time to look for other clients.

The secret in finding your star partner is to look for someone who serves your target market as well and discuss how both of you can add value to each other's' services. This is the reason why I focus a lot on the first C – Contact, in the previous section. You need to know clearly who is your target market and who is also serving your target market. Once you know who they are, it would be easier to find them in a networking event.

Attending a networking event will help you get contacts to help your business. But it will also allow you to help others. Whenever you meet someone, try to find out what help is that person looking for and see how best you can help them. For example, if I meet someone new, I would ask him is there anything I can help you in your business. This question normally opens a conversation where they will share more about their businesses and from the conversation, I will assess if I have the capability to help them, if not, I will ask myself is there someone I know that I can refer to them. This is my approach to helping business owners around me when I meet them in any networking events.

Believe In Yourself And the Work You Do!

Another lesson I have to learn so much these years is you must believe in the work you do before you can sell it to others. In a lot of sales training, the Trainer always say that the first person you must sell to is yourself.

I have seen a lot of business owners projecting a not-so-confident image when they are sharing what they do with their prospects. This is a terrible mistake because it will not help your business, instead, it will hurt your business because people will not have the confidence to engage your services or buy your product if you do not believe your services or products can help others first.

My suggestion is to always gather feedback and explore ways to improve your product or services so that you are sure that you have the best product for your target customers. This is the way to go! You must have a product that best suits your target market and there are no other places that provide as much value as yours. Knowing this, your confidence will shine, and people can feel that it just by listening to what you say.

To help you improve your confidence, even more, you should have stories at the back of your mind to be ready to share with anyone who you come across that your product and services can help. Stories are the best model to influence your target market so make sure you collect stories every day! Talk to your customers and attend networking events so that you can ask questions and let them reveal their pains to you. Of course, you must also tell stories how your products and services have helped others.

Telling stories is a skill but if you practice and tell them authentically and from the bottom of your heart, you will find yourself never have to sell!

Marketing That Makes Sales Irrelevant!

I used to think marketing is the same as sales but not really, marketing is what makes people know about you and your products. For example, if you are a management consultant, you may create a website to let people know that they can engage you as a consultant. Of course, you can also use other channels to market your services such as email marketing, facebook marketing, video marketing using YouTube, etc. The goal of marketing is to create interests in people to turn them into leads who are keen to purchase your products or services.

To me, sales is a transaction where you turn the leads into customers. Once you have generated leads, you can then follow-up with them so that they can decide if you are the best solution for them. Customers coming to your websites and buy things from you is also considered as sales although you are not meeting them personally.

There is a saying that great marketing makes sales irrelevant. This means your marketing is so powerful that people are queuing up to buy from you. This is mainly the results of great inbound marketing. Now I want to share with you that there are two types of marketing: inbound and outbound marketing.

Outbound marketing means that you are reaching out to your target market. For example, advertising on newspaper, making cold calls and distributing flyers are all outbound marketing. Outbound marketing has been very effective before the Internet era but now it has become annoying for most people as it is interruptive. Having said that, outbound marketing is still useful if you have the budget advertise because if you can increase your exposure rate to 1Million people, just 0.01% converts it means 100 new transactions. Therefore spamming will never go away because these companies are cashing in because of the huge coverage they have.

Inbound marketing is the most preferred type of marketing for most business owners because it means that people come to you rather than you reach out to them. If you ask any successful business owners, who have run their businesses for more than 10 years, a lot of them will tell you that word of mouth is their most effective marketing channel. Word of mouth or I call it referral marketing, is the best representative of inbound marketing.

Another type of inbound marketing is search engine marketing. Take for example Mary goes online and google for 'roof repair' as her roof is leaking. She then sees a list of websites that repair roofs in her area, she clicks on the first result and called the company. This example shows that customers go online and search for a solution then found what they want online. If customers found you online, it is inbound marketing for you because you are not actively reaching out to them about your services.

I would like to suggest that if you are new to business and would like inbound marketing to work for you, then study Search Engine Optimization (SEO) as well as Pay-Per-Click marketing as these channels are the core business generators for most businesses.

At the beginning of your business, perhaps you must do a lot of outbound marketing to get the attention. But you may not need to invest heavily in advertising on media. What you can do is to attend networking events and get to know people who you can collaborate and achieve a win-win scenario. For example, if you are a sales consultant and you met a branding consultant, both of you can attend each others' events to share some educational tips. This will not add any cost to your business and would most likely to generate leads for both of your businesses.

I started off as a Web Developer and later switched to a Trainer to teach people how to design their websites. It is when I am in the training business, I find that being a Trainer or Speaker has an advantage – higher perceive value. For example, some participants will come up to me after my training and ask me to design websites for them, and they will pay me. From the training I gave, people see the value and my expertise which is what I lack when I just provide web designing services back then.

What I want to share with you here is whatever you do, always find opportunities to speak in an event or share your expertise. This is one very big lesson I learn in business!

THE ONE THING THAT MAKES MARKETING IRRELEVANT!

Now that you know great marketing makes sales irrelevant. Do you know what makes marketing irrelevant? The answer is served with a heart and provide a good service.

I have seen many businesses started with a lot of focus on the customers, but slowly when they have too many customers by expanding too fast, their service quality falls, and eventually their businesses suffer. This is very common because in the beginning when you have very few customers, you will give each customer the most attention and care as much as you can. But this attitude most likely won't last especially when you have too many customers and leads to handle. If you didn't hire the right people to help you serve the customers, then your business and banding will be affected negatively.

Before you start a business, I just want you to think about the above scenario. Would you want to keep growing a business without consideration for customer service? I am sure your answer is no, and if you can, you would want to strike a perfect balance of giving the best customer experiences and growing your business.

The reason why I focus on customer service in this section is because it is the main thing that makes marketing irrelevant! If you really provide a good service to every one of your customers, you don't really need marketing because eventually, word of mouth will take over.

In todays' economy, it is easier to create great service because too many companies are spoiling the market by growing too fast or simply just care about the cash but not the customers! When I was doing web design for my customers, almost every customer will complain about their previous web designers as they just want to clinch the deal and move on to the next project as quickly as possible.

I just want to remind you that no matter how busy and successful you are in future, always take good care of your customers. They will, in turn, help you take care of your business (by spreading good words around).

I hope that you have gained at least one thing that you can implement after reading this book. This may be the last section of this book, but it is not the end. I would like to invite you to sign up my mailing list on the next page so that I can provide you with the latest insights and my future books as well.

I hope you enjoy this short read and this book has helped you to gain clarity in some areas through the sharing of my personal experiences. Now, go forth and create a meaningful business starting from your home! I believe there are many people out there who needs your services or products, do you think so?

SUBSCRIBE TO MY MAILING LIST!

Thank you so much for reading this book, and if you are keen to learn more and receive updates from me, you can consider joining my mailing list which you will receive:

- Videos on how to get started with your home business!

- Tools and resources that I use for my home business!

- Regular updates and tips on starting a profitable home business!

Subscribe at: http://homebusinesshelp.gr8.com/

I wish you all the best in your home business!

JJ&E
Your One Stop Business Service Center to Enhance Your Home Business

. . . .

Virtual Office Service

. . . .

★ **Company Registered Address**
(Use for ACRA record & keep your home address private)
- Prestigious CBD address!
- Email notification for mails collection, OR
- Forward mails to personal mailing address

★ **Mail Scanning Service**
- Mails will be scanned and forward via email

★ **Phone Answering Service**

★ **Fax Service**

★ **Meeting Room Rental**

Our Other Services:-

Registered Address Service start from **S$10** per month

* Visit our website for more details

Accounting Service
Bookkeeping, Tax & GST

Company Stamp
Customisable stamp, various sizes available

Company Registration
Free 1 Year Company Secretary & Starter Kits

Design & Printing
Logo, Name Card, Receipt Books & etc.

Corporate Secretary
AGM, AR, Annual Report, Government Compliance

CONTACT US :

Tel : **+65 6225 2028**   Website : **http://www.jje.sg**

Email : **jje888@gmail.com / info@jje.sg**

JJ&E 10 Anson Road #10-11 International Plaza, Singapore 079903

www.ingramcontent.com/pod-product-compliance
Lightning Source LLC
Chambersburg PA
CBHW021413170526
45164CB00002B/626